NFL TEAM STORIES

DENVER BRONCOS

By K.C. Kelley

Kaleidoscope
Minneapolis, MN

The Quest for Discovery Never Ends

This edition first published in 2021 by Kaleidoscope Publishing, Inc.

No part of this publication may be reproduced in whole or in part without written permission of the publisher.

For information regarding permission, write to Kaleidoscope Publishing, Inc.
6012 Blue Circle Drive
Minnetonka, MN 55343

Library of Congress Control Number
2020933947

ISBN
978-1-64519-227-5 (library bound)
978-1-64519-295-4 (ebook)

Printed in the United States of America.

FIND ME IF YOU CAN!

Bigfoot lurks within one of the images in this book. It's up to you to find him!

TABLE OF
CONTENTS

KICKOFF!

What's that horse doing on the field?!

Don't worry. Thunder is just doing its job. The Denver Broncos have just scored. The fans at Mile High Stadium are cheering. Then it's Thunder's turn. The horse's rider grabs a huge Broncos flag. Then Thunder charges into view. The fans cheer again!

Denver is in the West. Cowboys on horses are nothing new out there. At Broncos games, Thunder carries on the cowboy tradition. Broncos fans have seen Thunder run thousands of times! Let's meet the Broncos!

Thunder takes the field.

Chapter 1
Broncos History

By 1960, the NFL had become a really big deal. Many rich people wanted to own teams. But the NFL didn't want to add new teams. So a group of men started a new league. The Denver Broncos were part of the new American Football League. Ten AFL teams played during the 1960s. The Broncos were not one of the best teams, however. They never won more games than they lost.

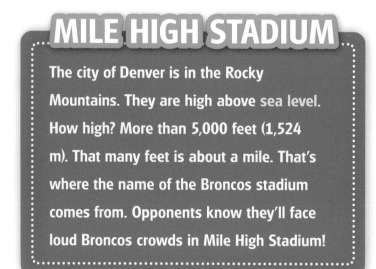

MILE HIGH STADIUM

The city of Denver is in the Rocky Mountains. They are high above sea level. How high? More than 5,000 feet (1,524 m). That many feet is about a mile. That's where the name of the Broncos stadium comes from. Opponents know they'll face loud Broncos crowds in Mile High Stadium!

In 1983, Denver got a player who could almost win games alone. The Broncos added star quarterback John Elway. Things turned around! Denver made the playoffs in Elway's first season. By 1986, he had led the team to the Super Bowl! To get there, he had to lead "The Drive."

In the AFC title game, Denver trailed Cleveland 20–13. Only five minutes were left. Elway took over

Elways drops back to pass during "The Drive."

Elway didn't do so well against the Giants in the Super Bowl.

98 yards from the **end zone**. He threw pass after pass. He kept the drive alive. The Broncos reached the five-yard line with 37 seconds left. Elway dropped back and looked for a target. He fired the ball to Mark Jackson. Touchdown! Denver won in **overtime**. The Broncos were off to the Super Bowl!

Unfortunately, Denver lost that game and two other Super Bowls in the 1980s.

Elway had chances to leave for other teams. But he and the Broncos stuck together. In 1997, the Broncos were back on top again. They won the AFC title game. Denver beat the Pittsburgh Steelers.

Back in the Super Bowl, Elway refused to lose again. In the fourth quarter, Denver was nearing the goal line. The team needed a first down. Elway carried the ball himself. He was going to get hit, but he dove anyway. He was smacked in midair! The 37-year-old QB spun like a helicopter! When he landed, he had the first down. The Broncos were **inspired** and went on to win. Elway was finally a Super Bowl champion!

Elway helicoptered for a huge first down.

Another great QB led the Broncos in the 2010s. Peyton Manning joined Denver in 2012. He was already a superstar and a champion. He brought his winning ways to Denver. In 2013, he also set a new NFL record with 55 TD passes.

The record was not enough. In Super Bowl XLVIII, Seattle's defense was just too good. Not even Manning could crack it. Denver lost 43-8. Two years later, Denver returned to the big game. Manning led them to a win in Super Bowl 50. (See page 14.)

SINGLE-SEASON
TD LEADERS

PLAYER	TD PASSES	YEAR
Peyton Manning	55	2013
Tom Brady	50	2007
Patrick Mahomes	50	2018

TIMELINE OF THE DENVER BRONCOS

1960

1960:
Denver plays its first game in AFL.

1977

1977:
Broncos make it to the Super Bowl.

1986

1986:
Denver wins AFC, but loses Super Bowl. Also lost two of next three Super Bowls.

1997

1997:
Broncos win Super Bowl XXXII, defeating the Green Bay Packers.

1998

1998:
Denver wins the Super Bowl again!

2013

2013:
Led by Peyton Manning, Broncos win AFC but lose Super Bowl.

2015

2015:
Broncos become the eighth team to win three Super Bowls. Denver defeats the Carolina Panthers.

CHAMPIONS!

Manning is the only QB to win a Super Bowl with two different teams.

The Broncos used big plays on defense to become Super Bowl 50 champions.

The game started well for Denver. Malik Jackson recovered a fumble in the end zone for a touchdown. In the second quarter, Jordan Norwood returned a punt 61 yards. That put the Broncos in great shape. Peyton Manning moved the team forward. Brandon McManus kicked his second field goal and Denver led 13–7.

Manning led another drive in the third quarter. He combined long passes with short running plays. Denver kicked another field goal. Then Denver's defense came through again. Von Miller sacked Carolina's Cam Newton. Newton fumbled! Denver got the ball on the four-yard line. Running back C.J. Anderson scored soon after.

The game ended with Denver on top 24–10. Manning earned his second Super Bowl trophy!

Chapter 2

Broncos All-Time Greats

Floyd Little played running back for Denver. He also helped build the team's stadium! He didn't grab a hammer, of course. Little was an All-American at Syracuse. He was drafted by Denver in 1967. Fans were so excited that they that helped raise money to build Mile High. In his nine seasons with the Broncos, he was one of the NFL's best players. Denver fans loved his hard-nosed running style.

On December 20, 1975, Little played his last game for the Broncos. The team lost, but fans stormed the field. They carried their hero off the gridiron in honor of his great career.

Little rumbles against the Cincinnati Bengals.

FUN FACT

The Broncos wore the helmets shown here until 1997. Then the team changed its logo.

Elway was a great runner, too.

THE ELWAY CROSS

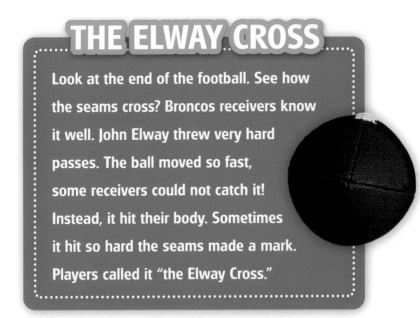

Look at the end of the football. See how the seams cross? Broncos receivers know it well. John Elway threw very hard passes. The ball moved so fast, some receivers could not catch it! Instead, it hit their body. Sometimes it hit so hard the seams made a mark. Players called it "the Elway Cross."

John Elway was a Broncos legend. He was almost a Baltimore Colt. That NFL team chose him first in the 1983 NFL Draft. Elway and his parents did not want him playing for the Colts, however. The star QB said he would switch to baseball! So the Colts traded him to Denver. Broncos fans enjoyed the result. Elway led the team to five Super Bowls. He thrilled fans with his strong passing arm. He could also scramble out of trouble!

Peyton Manning also moved from the Colts to the Broncos. In 2012, he joined Denver after 14 seasons with the Colts. He was already an NFL star. His leadership made the Broncos into winners again.

A pair of great offensive players helped Elway win Denver's first Super Bowl. Rod Smith spent 12 seasons with the Broncos. He had at least 70 catches in nine of those years! In Super Bowl XXXIII, Smith scored on an 80-yard TD catch.

Running back Terrell Davis had the right nickname. "T.D." led the NFL with 23 TDs in 1998. He was also the fourth runner ever to top 2,000 yards in a season. He scored three times in Super Bowl XXXII.

FUN FACT

Terrell Davis was on the NFL's All-Decade Team for the 1990s.

BRONCOS

RECORDS

These players piled up the best stats in Broncos history. The numbers are career records through the 2019 season.

Total TDs: Rod Smith, 71

TD Passes: John Elway, 300

Passing Yards: John Elway, 51,475

Rushing Yards: Terrell Davis, 7,607

Receptions: Rod Smith, 849

Points: Jason Elam, 1,786

Sacks: Von Miller, 106

Chapter 3

Broncos Superstars

Sometimes teams find surprise stars. In 2017, Phillip Lindsay had 1,474 rushing yards for Colorado. He was surprised when no NFL teams chose him in the draft. But he didn't let that stop him. Lindsay tried out for the Broncos. They took a chance on him. He made the most of it. Lindsay ran for 107 yards in his second game! By the next week, he was the starter. Lindsay ended up with 1,037 yards. That was the most ever by a rookie who had not been drafted. Fans loved his hard-nosed running style, too.

THE NFL DRAFT

Each spring, NFL teams grow. At the NFL Draft, they choose college players. Each team chooses in turn. The teams with bad records choose first. The best teams choose last. That helps keep things fair. Most top players, like Von Miller, were high draft picks. Denver's Phillip Lindsay showed you don't have to be drafted to be a star.

Off the field, Von Miller looks like a teacher. He wears thick glasses with dark frames. On the field, he looks very different! The Denver linebacker teaches opponents a lesson. Don't try to get past him!

Miller plays his best in big games. In Super Bowl 50, he had to chase down Carolina's Cam Newton. Newton was big and fast. So was Miller. Late in the game, Miller charged around the end. He reached out a huge hand. SMACK! He knocked the ball out of Newton's hand. Denver pounced on the ball. Miller was named the Super Bowl MVP!

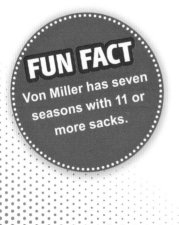

FUN FACT
Von Miller has seven seasons with 11 or more sacks.

Joseph Jones (43) and Von Miller get ready to make a tackle.

On April 23, 2019, the Broncos might have found their future. The team chose Drew Lock of Missouri in the NFL Draft. Big and tall, Lock ran Missouri's offense for four seasons. Could he become Denver's next starter?

The 2019 season began and Lock was on the bench. In December, he became the starter. He won four of his first five games! Against Houston, Lock threw three TD passes. Coaches were impressed with his calm style. Look for Drew to "lock" up the position!

Courtland Sutton

Drew Lock hands off to Phillip Lindsay.

Courtland Sutton will be a key target for him. Sutton led Denver in catches, TD catches, and receiving yards.

Denver has a championship history. Can Lock, Sutton, and other stars keep it going? Thunder can't wait to start running again!

BEYOND
THE BOOK

After reading the book, it's time to think about what you learned. Try the following exercises to jumpstart your ideas.

RESEARCH

FIND OUT MORE. Where would you go to find out more about your favorite NFL teams and players? Check out NFL.com, of course. Each team also has its own website. What other sports information sites can you find? See if you can find other cool facts about your favorite team.

CREATE

GET ARTISTIC. Each NFL team has a logo. The Broncos logo shows a horse rearing up. Get some art materials and try designing your own Broncos logo. Or create a new team and make a logo for it. What colors would you choose? How would you draw the mascot?

DISCOVER

GO DEEP! As this book shows, the Broncos play home games a mile above sea level. Read more about playing sports that high. How does it affect players? How does it affect the ball? How do teams adapt to playing in these conditions?

GROW

GET OUT AND PLAY! You don't need to be in the NFL to enjoy football. You just need a football and some friends. Play touch or tag football. Or you can hang cloth flags from your belt; grab the belt and make the "tackle." See who has the best arm to be quarterback. Who is the best receiver? Who can run the fastest? Time to play football!

RESEARCH NINJA

Visit *www.ninjaresearcher.com/2275* to learn how
to take your research skills and book report writing to the next level!

RESEARCH ··

DIGITAL LITERACY TOOLS

SEARCH LIKE A PRO
Learn about how to use search engines to find useful websites.

FACT OR FAKE?
Discover how you can tell a trusted website from an untrustworthy resource.

TEXT DETECTIVE
Explore how to zero in on the information you need most.

SHOW YOUR WORK
Research responsibly— learn how to cite sources.

WRITE ···

GET TO THE POINT
Learn how to express your main ideas.

PLAN OF ATTACK
Learn prewriting exercises and create an outline.

DOWNLOADABLE REPORT FORMS

Further Resources

BOOKS

Buckley, James Jr. *Von Miller and the Denver Broncos: Super Bowl 50*. Minneapolis: Bearport Publishing, 2016.

Jacobson, Ryan. *Phillip Lindsay: Rise of a Hometown Legend*. Minneapolis: Lake 7 Creative, 2019.

Whiting, Jim. *Denver Broncos (NFL Today)*. Mankato, Minn.: Creative Paperbacks, 2019.

WEBSITES

FACTSURFER

Factsurfer.com gives you a safe, fun way to find more information.

1. Go to www.factsurfer.com.
2. Enter "Denver Broncos" into the search box and click 🔍
3. Select your book cover to see a list of related websites.

Glossary

drafted: chosen by an NFL team from college. Von Miller was drafted No. 1 by the Broncos in 2011.

end zone: area at each end of the field where touchdowns are scored. Drew Lock dove into the end zone for six points!

fumble: a ball dropped by a ball carrier. Denver was in trouble after Phillip Lindsay lost the ball on a fumble.

gridiron: a nickname for a football field. Old-time fields had many more lines on them. People thought the fields looked like cooking gridirons.

inspired: pushed to do better. Peyton Manning's hard work inspired his teammates to work hard, too.

overtime: extra time added to a game after a 60-minute game ends in a tie. After tying Pittsburgh 10–10, Denver scored in overtime to win 13–10.

sacked: tackled the QB behind the line of scrimmage. Von Miller sacked Tom Brady and pushed the Patriots back nine yards.

sea level: a height of land equal to the level of the ocean. Denver is more than a mile above sea level.

Index

PHOTO CREDITS

About the Author

K.C. Kelley is the author of more than 100 sports books for kids. He has written about football, baseball, basketball, soccer, and many other popular games. He lives in Santa Barbara, California, with his family.